Lawrence's Muse

Lawrence's Muse
Jessie Chambers Wood through her own writing
Ed. Clive Leivers

Published in 2023 by Five Leaves,
14a Long Row, Nottingham, NG1 2DH
www.fiveleaves.co.uk
www.fiveleavesbookshop.co.uk

ISBN 978-1-915434-08-1

Printed in Great Britain

Lawrence's Muse

Jessie Chambers Wood
through her own writing

edited by Clive Leivers

Five Leaves Publications
www.fiveleaves.co.uk

Acknowledgements

Clive Leivers, 1938 - 2022

Clive Leivers became chairman of the Haggs Farm Preservation Society soon after it was founded by Ann Howard, Jessie Chambers' niece in 1986. His affinity to the Haggs went back to his childhood. He was born and brought up in Underwood and his grandad was born at Haggs Farm. Clive credited his upbringing in the rural environment of Underwood for his love of the countryside, love of music and love of literature. As chair of the Society, Clive worked tirelessly to raise awareness of Haggs Farm and remind people of its literary significance, never wavering in his aim of ensuring its conservation and maybe one day its restoration. He edited two books, *Miriam's Farm* and *Lawrence's Muse: Jessie Chambers Wood through her own writing*, both definitive reads for anyone wanting to find out more about the history of the Haggs, D.H. Lawrence and Jessie Chambers.

The Society is grateful to Nottingham University and University College London for providing copies of documents and granting permission to publish the items listed in the bibliography.

Dr Barbara Kearns of the University of Sydney kindly supplied copies of Jessie's *Adelphi* article and the *Times Literary Supplement* review.

Thanks are also due to Martin Allen for his agreement to the publication of those items still under copyright.

Contents

Introduction

In 'Autobiographical Sketch', D.H. Lawrence described Jessie Chambers as "the chief friend of my youth." Born on 29th January 1887, a year younger than Lawrence, Jessie was eleven years old when her family left Eastwood to go to live at Haggs Farm, Underwood. Lawrence became a regular visitor and developed a close bond with the whole family and in particular, Jessie, whom he portrayed as Miriam in *Sons and Lovers*. Lawrence credited Jessie with launching his literary career, but their relationship broke down for many reasons. Afterwards, Jessie went on to become a teacher, but always continued writing and studying. She married Jack Wood in 1915 and, after Lawrence's death, wrote her memoir, *A Personal Record*, which was published in 1935.

The idea for this book originated with Malcolm Pittock, who had been given copies of letters from Jessie Wood to Dorothy Plowman written between 1930 and 1942 which were in the possession of Mrs Greta Plowman, the daughter-in-law of Max Plowman. Malcolm suggested that these should be published together with other unpublished writing by Jessie, including her short story 'The Bankrupt' and reviews of *A Personal Record* which were mentioned in the Plowman correspondence.

In pursuing this proposal, other articles and letters by Jessie came to light: postcards and letters to her sister May, an article explaining her adherence to pacifism, and two colour sketches she had drawn. These give new insights into Jessie's beliefs and interests and provide evidence of the range of her talents as writer and artist.

Haggs Farm Preservation Society

The Society was formed in 1986 to encourage the preservation of the Haggs Farm buildings and to reinforce the vital importance of Haggs Farm in the formative years of D.H. Lawrence's development as a writer. The aims of the Society are: to promote interest in and, as opportunity arises, to be actively involved with the preservation of the buildings, with the aim of securing some form of public access; and to research and publicise the history of the farm, its tenants and the Lawrence connection.

Chapter One: Plowman and Pacifism

Max Plowman

Plowman was the only soldier actively serving in the First World War who became a conscientious objector. His pacifism was lifelong: he became a friend of Canon Dick Sheppard who founded the Peace Pledge Union in which Max became an active member.

He was also a literary journalist, friend of Middleton Murry and editor of the literary journal *The Adelphi*. He had a particular passion for the work of William Blake, and his article in *The Adelphi* in March 1930, 'William Blake and the Imagination of Truth', inspired Jessie Wood to write an appreciative letter to the author, whom she recognised as the ideal person to guide her in the writing of her memoir of Lawrence. This was the start of their relationship.

Only one of Jessie's letters to Plowman survives (Letter Four below) but several written by Max to her are included in his collected letters, *Bridge into the Future*, edited by his wife Dorothy.

The first of these, dated May 25th, 1930, does not refer to any autobiographical project but commiserates about the impertinence of journalists who were hounding her following Lawrence's death. The next, written six days later, makes it clear that Jessie had started on what was to become *A Personal Record* and had sent an outline to Plowman, who offered some practical advice. By 2nd July that year Jessie had completed an interim draft which she sent to Plowman, who gave an encouraging response but thought that the account of her relationship with DHL — "beautifully recalled" — stopped too soon. Three days later she sent the final chapter, which Max saw as "completing the circle & mak[ing] everything explicable."

A Personal Record, though essentially complete by July 1930, was not published until 1935. Jessie was reluctant to see her work published and allowed Plowman to keep it until 1933. The impetus for further revision and subsequent publication then came from Emile Delavenay, who was writing a thesis about Lawrence and approached Jessie for information. There was also further encouragement from David Chambers and Janko Lavrin, Professor of Russian at University College Nottingham, who taught Jessie Russian and suggested how the memoir might be organised. By 1934

Jessie had decided on publication and turned again to Plowman for advice and assistance.

The book was published the following year with a short prefatory note under the initials M.P., which very probably refer to Plowman, although in Letter Three below Jessie expresses regret that the book did not include an acknowledgement of his association with it.

Malcolm Pittock

Letter One

Woodthorpe
Nottingham

Dec 4th 1930

My dear Mrs Plowman,

We are in the Christmas month and should like to renew very heartily our invitation to you all to spend some days with us during our holiday.

I should have written earlier, but a fortnight ago I slipped on the landing step and hurt the muscles of my back so badly that I could not come downstairs for a week. I am a little "invalidish" still, but shall be quite recovered long before Christmas.

Our holiday begins on Dec 19th and lasts exactly two weeks. We shall be happy to have you all for a few days if you can spare the time, and dare brave a journey north in midwinter.

The weather is the great "if", but we are as likely to have fine weather at Christmas as at Midsummer.

We shall very much enjoy showing you my old homestead and its setting, and my husband's countryside with its quite different charm. So, if you possibly can, do come. At present we have made no plans at all, so that, provided we know a little in advance, any days within the fortnight will suit us, and I think there are convenient short date tickets issued by which one can travel on fast trains.

I hope you are all well. Is Piers very excited about Christmas? Jack says the Christmas fever is making itself felt in school.

With kindest regards from both
Yours very sincerely

Comment

Jessie's first contact with Max Plowman was around May 1930. Her approach to Max about her memoir had obviously led to friendship with his wife Dorothy as well as with him, and she obviously wished to strengthen the acquaintance with an invitation to visit. The old homestead was the Haggs, which was visited by the Plowmans at some time (see Letter Six).

Letter Two

43 Breckhill Road
Woodthorpe
Nottingham

June 2nd 1931

Dearest Dorothy

I shall never get down onto paper all the things I want to say in this letter. First — your lovely 'Threnody' — thank you so much for letting me see it. It is so fine to be able to get one's deep inner experience crystallised into external beauty. The phrase that holds the fullest significance for me is —

And yet… never quite unknowable to those who are <u>not afraid of suffering</u> — it seems to be the inevitable gateway to further life.

Then I am so delighted with Mr Plowman's article on 'God — Faith — and Mr Murry'. Its forthrightness is sheer joy to me, and every word is immediately understandable, and just states my own faith in life. The last two paragraphs are beyond comment — they hold what is the staff of life for me (when I am strong enough and brave enough to see it). The two paragraphs on p254 recall very curiously my last bit of correspondence with JMM. In the last letter he wrote to me (I wish I had thought to show it to you, but you shall see it later) he says "F (this is the central fact about her) is an innocent woman, an Eve who has never eaten of the fruit of the Tree." I still have the envelope on which I scribbled the rough draft of my reply. I wrote "Your letter raises into clear relief what from the first I dimly guessed. It seems to me that L and F were separated by some thousands of years of human development. F is 'innocent' in a pre-moral sense — L on the other hand was essentially super-moral, it was his business to achieve the true Beyond Good and Evil. The tie with his mother cut the ground from under his feet and prevented him from fulfilling his latent possibilities. It seems to me that the essence of the conflict between him and F lay in the confusion of Beyond Good and Evil with the <u>Before</u> Good and Evil. The Eve who has not eaten of the Tree and the Adam who stands at the very threshold of a new humanity must inevitably conflict with one another. Precisely there, I think, lay L's sense of sin.

I am sure DHL tried to go back to Eden instead of forward to the City of God. I knew it at the time, although not in those words, and I knew within myself that such a return can never be made; I also knew that he had to see his experiment through to the end. The great thing I was waiting to see was whether, having realised he was going in the wrong direction, he would have the power to make the complete right about face and turn towards the City of God. I felt absolutely sure that such a change was taking place within him towards the end, and sometimes I awoke suddenly in the very early morning hours with a mind full of the thought of it. Could such a miracle happen — and how could it happen? Then his death came like ruin in the midst of it all, but I don't think now that it was ruin — perhaps another kind of fulfilment. All this seems to me so closely knitted in with the argument of the very fine article that it is worthwhile to tell you about it.

While on the subject just let me make a remark on H. L. Salmon's 'Lawrence and a Sense of the Whole'. I still think that Waldo Frank was right. If L could have attained a "sense of the whole" it might have been his salvation. Incidentally, that seeking of "extraordinary moments" was one of our fundamental points of difference. I could not endure the idea of life as a succession of "extraordinary moments" with immense stretches of the most awful desert between. We differed finally and fatally upon that very point — (I believe it comes up in *Sons and Lovers*). It was the best he could hope for — and to me simply unendurable.

And now to thank you both most heartily for the parcel of books that came yesterday, and especially the one inscribed to me, which will always bring up the happiest memories and associations, as well as give me great joy in itself. *The Possessed* I shall read again. Is Murry's preface new for this edition? There are one or two points with which I don't agree, particularly where he says that Kirilov was another Jesus. I cannot understand JMM's conception of Jesus, neither do I think that Dostoevsky could see no difference between Good and Evil. Prince Mirsky's book is a beautiful volume, we shall both enjoy it immensely.

One request — may we keep them quite a long time because Jack in particular has so little time for reading just now, but we will of course take great care of them and return them safely when we have read them.

On Saturday we were taking our little niece a ride in the car and we wandered into the country of *The Rainbow*. I was astonished to see how pretty it is — you must see it the next time you are here. On Sunday we were in Sherwood Forest and saw the great oak under whose branches Robin Hood spread his generous table. We thought Piers might like the picture. That is another thing to see on your next visit.

I quite forgot when we were at the farm to ask mother for the family photographs, but it would have been difficult to find them by candlelight. I'll get her to look out the few relics I believe she still has of DHL for next time. The old people will be delighted to see you both again.

I have started the revision of 'Judas Iscariot'.

I should very much like to have a long letter from you when the time and the mood come together. I feel I have said scarcely a word of sympathy, with all that you have gone through lately, but it is really beyond words; but you <u>do</u> know I feel greatly privileged to be able to share it with you.

With love from both of us to you all

Comment

In the six months since the previous letter Dorothy Plowman and Jessie had forged a close relationship, with Jessie writing to "dearest Dorothy." The Plowmans were now clearly aware of Jessie's interests and the highs and lows of her relationship with Lawrence; Dorothy's 'Threnody' and the article by Max obviously struck a chord.

It is a little strange that Jessie was surprised by the landscape in which *The Rainbow* was set since she had walked through it with DHL and friends at least once from Eastwood via Ilkeston to the Hemlock Stone at Bramcote. (*A Personal Record* p41)

By this date the Plowmans had paid at least one visit to the Woods and had been to meet Jessie's parents — "the old people".

Letter Three

June 18th 1935

My dear Dorothy,

The routine of schooldays gives me leisure once more; I can never get down to things in a holiday week. This holiday has been a specially busy one since Jack was taking part in the Historical Pageant that Nottingham has seen fit to hold. There is plenty of historical material in our town, and Jack has been a gentleman attendant on King Charles in the Raising of the Standard episode, and made a surprisingly successful Cavalier, resplendent in plum-coloured velvet, wig, and ostrich plumes. The setting was a beautiful natural arena, with an Elizabethan mansion for a background. It has been quite interesting and amusing, and our jaunt to the sea-side at the end of the week finished off the holiday in good style.

We were both very sorry you were not able to come down this Whitsuntide but we understand perfectly how you were feeling.

This spring has been the cruellest I remember, from the weather point of view. But I believe we have actually fared better here than you have in the south; we did not have such severe frosts, and the rain came in time to save the garden. The projected orchard at the bottom of the lawn is now an accomplished fact, and was gay with crocuses and daffodils early in the year. Our Van Fleet rose is now in bloom; I wonder if yours is.

I'm so glad you liked the butter; I did want you to taste it.

We have been enjoying it tremendously this spring. By the curious working of the Milk Marketing Board, the Ling's Lane milk was "surplus", and there was nothing to do but turn it into butter. They are lucky in having a most wonderful "butter cow"; five minutes after milking there is thick yellow cream, so that accounts for the rich colour of the butter. I must tell you also about a wonderful little hen they have had this spring. She was observed to disappear each day during feeding time, and finally was traced to a nest behind the straw-stack, where she was sitting on seventeen eggs — all her own laying, of course the marvel was that she could cover them all, being only a small hen. The next day they found her with a nest full of chickens, sixteen hatched out, and the seventeenth cheeping in its shell. The mother herself was one of a self-set brood. I don't quite know why, but the thought of this little hen somehow warms my heart.

I've really felt <u>very</u> happy about the book since its publication. Like you, I was most disappointed that your names were not associated with it, and I assure you, Jack and I would have felt honoured to have them there. I was indeed distressed because I felt I had bungled rather badly, accepting the publishers' commercially sounding note in the first place. But it all came right in the end. No, I have not had the notices forwarded to me. In the first place I didn't quite know how to proceed about it, and again I felt quite nervous about them until Max so kindly sent me the *Times Lit. Supp.* notice which was most unexpectably good. So far as I have seen, that review is the only one that goes at all below the surface, and is by far the best. I liked L. A. G. Strong's in *Time and Tide* and Sylvia Lynd's in the *News Chronicle*. But what I do very much appreciate is the fact that the book has been treated seriously. I can't tell you the relief it is to have it definitely done; a sense of lightness, a freeing from an old burden, and even new possibilities.

I mustn't forget to tell you that I have had a letter of appreciation from Lady Ottoline Morrell — I'll show it to you some day, the most extraordinary calligraphy I've ever seen, rather beautiful in its way, but I wouldn't care to read many pages of it. Then a Polish professor has sent a most enthusiastic letter — from Cracow this — saying it is the best book on Lawrence he has read, and that he intends to review it in a Polish journal. He asks if I realise that there is still a new life in sight as he became a writer of English at 60, and now at 72 is full of readiness for new adventures. He offers to send me what he has written in Polish on L; and as I have a friend who is a Pole, I have thanked him and accepted his offer. I have also had a long account of his own student days from a teacher who was in class with me at the Pupil-Teacher centre — he remembers Lawrence well, and is evidently a great admirer of his work. That is the sum-total of correspondence it has called forth so far — quite interesting. I haven't told father and mother about the book. Somehow I can't overcome my reluctance to talk about it to them. I feel it is rather a shame to deny them any joy they might feel, but on the other hand, the reading of it would awaken old unhappy memories that I think are best left undisturbed. So no one knows but David, my older brother has apparently not seen anything in the local press.

Father and Mother have not been too well this spring. They miss the shelter of the farm. Down there in the hollow they never felt the east wind, but here they get it full blast. I hope when the summer weather really comes and they can get out more, then they will get back some of their old resiliency.

I think you have decided very wisely in letting Piers go away to school. The parting will be a wrench but I think Piers will find it easier to make those inevitable readjustments, among strangers. What a strange and little understood element of growth it is — this necessary withdrawal from one's own people and particularly one's parents. My mother tried to keep her brood in the nest for too long; we have all suffered from it in some degree, but it has affected the boys more vitally than the girls. Why is that, I wonder?

I'm exceedingly glad to hear that Max is well away on a book at last; these sterile patches can be devastating. May the waters of inspiration well up deep and strong. And you? I hope you [have?] a renewal of energy that often follows the final making of a difficult decision.

We still hope that the summer will provide an opportunity for a meeting. If you feel there is one any time, do let us know. I wish for many reasons that we were likely to come to *The Adelphi* Summer School, but the date cuts our holiday in two and I don't feel that I ought to persuade Jack to forgo what he most prizes in his four weeks of freedom, the liberty to go where and when he will. His nose is kept to the grindstone very thoroughly right through the year. It would do us good, particularly the meeting with various people, and if Jack wanted to come I should be delighted, but I would [not?] have him come unwillingly. So you see how it is. Perhaps you might manage a week-end in the autumn — it might help to relieve the first [loneliness?] of Piers absence at school. I do hope he will be happy there; we read a fine account of Bedales some time ago. What a world we may enjoy when life is so framed that that kind of education is the norm, and available to all. In the schools we know, boys of Piers' age have already passed beyond us, and the gates of "industry" have closed upon them.

Jack unites with me in sending our warmest greetings to you all,
Ever yours affectionately.

Comment

The pageant in which Jack appeared was held in Wollaton Park with its Elizabethan mansion as a backdrop. Jessie's love of gardening and her background as a farmer's daughter are apparent. Lings Lane Farm was in Keyworth where both Jack and May Holbrook taught and where Jack's sister lived.

This letter provides the first account of Jessie's reaction to the publication of *A Personal Record*. (Chapter 2 contains a selection of reviews, including that in the *Times Literary Supplement*.)

The Polish professor was Wincenty Lutoslawski; Jessie's first letter to him was in June 1935 and the correspondence continued until October.

Bedales, the school attended by Piers Plowman, was founded in 1893 on progressive principles with as much emphasis on craft education and outdoor activities as formal classwork — a philosophy which was attractive to the Plowmans, and also apparently to Jessie.

Letter Four

43 Breck Hill Rd
Woodthorpe
Nottingham

Jan 22nd 1936

Dear Mr Plowman

We both thank you very much for your book, both because it is yours and because it deals with the subject that of all questions today lies nearest our hearts. You don't need any convincing from me on that score.

Reading through the essays again I am grateful for your clear exposition of what so-called "war" is nowadays — during the last war I was haunted by the horror of opposing human bodies to war machines, but what of nowadays! 'The Test of Magnanimity' just indicates the job that is facing us, because alternative methods to war have got to be found, and only the insistence of the people who are determined not to use war as a means will cause them to be found.

It's frightfully difficult but where there's a will there's a way. I like immensely the chapter on the religious basis and subscribe in humility to all that is implied there — it's a great ideal, worth all the effort of which one is capable. "Pacifism is an adventure of the human spirit." True, it is really the only adventure of these days. The opposite is confession of failure, of inability to grapple with the supreme problem of our time. And it's good to end with laughter, and the admission that war is a fool's game. With really sane people the idea of war would be laughed out of court.

We shall show your book to all our friends and do our best to get people interested in the cause. Thanks once again.

Yours ever
Jessie Wood [Chambers]
"Miriam"

Comment

This is the only letter from Jessie to Max that survives in the Plowman archives held by University College London. It was sent in response to the receipt of Plowman's book *The Faith Called Pacifism*.

Letter Five

43 Breck Hill Road
Woodthorpe
Nottingham

Nov 1st 1937

Dear Dorothy,

This is just to tell you how shocked and grieved we both are at the news of Canon Sheppard's death, and to send a word of sympathy to you and Max in what we know must be a most grievous personal loss.

I thank God that I saw Dick Sheppard at Swanwick. Unless I had actually seen him I could never have believed there was such a man. It will always be a great inspiration to me to have seen a man who really loved his fellow men.

One hardly dares to think of the loss to the cause. But speaking personally to have lost Dick Sheppard is an occasion for a re-dedication of myself to the service [of?] that for which he gave himself unstintingly. With greetings to you both from both [of us]

Comment

Canon Dick Sheppard was the founder of the Peace Pledge Union and a close friend and colleague of Max, who was also involved in its foundation. He attended rallies in Derbyshire earlier in 1937, one of which Jessie refers to.

Letter Six

Nov 19th 1942

My dear Dorothy,

I have finished Max's book this week, and I want to thank you (and him) for it from the bottom of my heart. It is a very fine book, and shows a Christian in the truest sense of the word. It must have been a great joy to you to gather these essays together and make such a beautiful book of them. It is the finest memorial to Max that could be imagined.

It may perhaps interest you to know the order in which I read the book. First came the Editor's Note; then the Essays and last the Introduction, which is quite good in its way. At long last J.M.M. seems to have broken his inveterate habit of talking about himself. Or was it perhaps [next line not readable] who writes the *Pacifist Commentary*? I often wonder. It was in his column that I first saw a notice of Max's work and forthwith I went to my newsagent and ordered it. After several fruitless calls, they asked whether it was being advertised. Then finally came your kind notice that it was to be published in October.

A few weeks ago I had a copy of Ellis Roberts' *Biography of Dick Sheppard*. I wonder if you've seen it. It is a huge book. The author seemed so anxious to tell everything that he made no distinction between grain and chaff. All the time (which wasn't much) that I spent over it, I kept wishing for a winnowing machine to separate the good corn from the chaff. Surely Dick Sheppard should have a better biographer. I quite agreed with Lord Ponsonby's review of it, which he called <u>Mr Roberts' Chestnuts</u>.

When the essays are of such a high standard it is difficult to pick out a favourite. The very first I read quite a number of years ago now was the one entitled 'William Blake and the Imagination of Truth'. Incidentally it was that essay that brought me into contact with Max. I mentioned it in a letter, and he replied thanking me for my kind words about his essay. I always regard it as a marvellous chance that I came into contact with Max when I did. Or should I say more truly that it was the guiding hand of God? He would say so, I'm sure. After that I think

I like 'The Nature of Modern War'. That sums up the whole situation. I fully appreciate the distinction Max draws between renouncing war, and resisting war. In that connection I thought Laurence Housman's review in *Peace News* was very good.

Of the literary essays of course the *Hamlet* one stands at the top. It is a very fine essay, and it's just right that the *Macbeth* follows it straight away. It was a great joy to read them again, and will be many times in the future. I should like to tell you how I agree with a sentence in your Editor's note. You say Max was "most at home among the great princes of art, or the saints of God — who are in truth the same." I have enjoyed it thoroughly, and you must be very proud of him.

I still take *Peace News* and rejoiced that they had cleared the debt on Dick Sheppard House. I am glad that my humble £1 helped. You would be sure to be at the concert held at Friends' House on Oct 31st. I hope you had the joy of seeing Piers play his part among The Adelphi Players. He must be a handsome fellow by now. Please remember me to him.

I suppose it must be a great grief to you to leave Langham, the more so because of the reason. I should hate to live near a military aerodrome myself. It is rather a shame they couldn't find any other spot, but then in times like these, we're entirely in the hands of the military.

I don't know where to send this letter, but hope it will be forwarded to wherever you are.

We are both very well. Jack has to go on duty fire-watching one night in eight. It is his duty night tonight. He gets to school nowadays by bus, which passes our house. When he comes home at midday, he cycles in the afternoon. But during the darkest months of the year they have a shortened dinner hour, which doesn't allow him to get home. He gets his midday meal [line missing?]

I think our food has been managed extremely well by Lord Woolton — he has earned the VC, I'm sure.

Father still lives alone and looks after himself. He is in his 80th year. I just make a fruit pie for him on Sunday, and he fetches it. He is a great reader, and that helps him out. I wonder if your parents are alive?

David left Wollaton and returned to Ashby de la Zouch just over 2 years ago. Since the petrol restriction we don't see much of him. He came over one evening in the spring. His errand was to beg clothing coupons from Father. They had spent all his on Ann, who is 14 years old now. It seems incredible doesn't it. She was such a wee thing when you and Max and Piers came to visit us. Do you remember how, when we were at Haggs Farm, Ann and Max walked hand in hand, and then I saw that Max had picked her up and was carrying her. I am so glad we met when we did and had those <u>good</u> times together.

Jack joins in sending best wishes and love to you and Piers.
Yours ever,
Jessie

Comment

Since the previous letter Jessie had suffered a stroke in April 1939, and it was several months before she was sufficiently recovered to return home. Max Plowman had died in June 1941, so the lives of both women had been severely affected. But by now Jessie was well enough to resume the correspondence, and Dorothy Plowman had produced a collection of Max's essays as a tribute to his memory. This was *The Right To Live* which Jessie so much appreciated.

The other major change in Dorothy's life was the move from the family home at Langham in Essex because of the building of a military aerodrome nearby. Langham had been purchased by Middleton Murry in 1934 and established as a pacifist community centre. The Plowmans appear to have moved there around November 1939 from their previous home on Erskine Hill in Golders Green, London, and among other activities Max ran a hostel for conscientious objectors who were working on adjacent land.

Dorothy Plowman had written how much her family had enjoyed meeting Jessie's parents (see Letter Seven) and Jessie now reports on her father's health and her brother David's career moves, and she recalls the good times enjoyed when the Plowmans visited, including a trip to the Haggs. David's daughter Ann, who Jessie mentions, was a founding member of the Haggs Farm Preservation Society in 1985.

The Adelphi

The Adelphi or *New Adelphi* was an English literary journal founded by John Middleton Murry. Max Plowman became editor in 1938. The magazine published several short stories by D.H. Lawrence. It also published essays on a wide variety of topics.

Jessie's commitment to the pacifist cause is evident in her letters to the Plowmans, and two years earlier in March 1936, she had written to Willie Hopkin suggesting that pacificism was the "chief thing worth working for just now". She obviously wanted to share the reasons for that conviction with a wider audience, which she did in this contribution to *The Adelphi*.

The Adelphi, November 1938

Prompt Corner

Under this heading, readers are invited to "prompt" where necessary, or to contribute significant ideas that do not call for full-length treatment. 'Prompt Corner' offers an open forum for every kind of sincere conviction that can be expressed in a few words.

1918-1938 — Twenty Years After

Whenever I speak about pacifism I am obliged to go back to the beginning and find out what it was that turned me into a convinced opponent of war. My case, no doubt, is typical of thousands, perhaps millions of others.

We were engaged and looking forward to getting married when the war descended on us like a bolt from the blue, for I had grown up in the serene assumption that war between "civilised" nations was now only a matter of history. All that was generous in us responded to the call for self-sacrifice. My fiancé told me that columns of marching men kept passing in front of his eyes all the time he was at work. I understood how he felt. In his place I should have felt and acted just the same. It looked like a clear summons to duty. I didn't dream of holding him back, but I held my breath while he told me what it was he thought of joining, and was immeasurably relieved when he mentioned the medical services. Being quite unpolitically-minded, I had not even heard of pacifism; but the idea that the man who was to be my husband should come to me with the blood of his fellows on his hands was unthinkable.

He joined up early in 1915, and before he went to the Front we were married. He was granted four days leave for the occasion. We saw one another again a few weeks later when he arrived unexpectedly in the small hours for two days leave, and then he was gone overseas — only to France, it is true, but it might have been a thousand miles away. However, we were sure the war couldn't last more than another year at the most. The delicate fabric of modern finance would never stand the strain, so the experts assured us.

It was sixteen months before I saw my husband again. He came striding towards me along the railway platform, burdened with all the paraphernalia of a soldier on leave from active service — tin hat, tin mug, and half-a-hundred precious oddments, necessary bits of household gear. It struck me that one-half of a soldier's life consists of a pathetic domesticity. But he was gay and confident.

"Shall we get real democracy at the end of the war, do you think?" I asked him.

"We've got to," he replied. "It's the democracies that are fighting the war; the democracies will have the settling of it."

That was in 1916. We know better now.

"I may be lousy," he told me apologetically, "all the fellows are: there's no help for it. I spent half the night de-lousing before I left the base; but I'm bound to have nits."

In the bathroom he stripped and pitched his uniform and underclothing in one bundle through the window. It was a frosty night. "There's nothing like cold for killing livestock," he said.

He seemed bursting to talk. I could feel the relief it gave him to tell of the crazy inversion of ordinary human values: it helped him to preserve a sane perspective. His contempt for the military mind was boundless. In the army, capacity to do a particular job meant the certainty of not being given that job to do. "If a man's a first-rate boot-mender he's set to pick up match-ends and litter…" He spoke of rats the size of a full-grown cat cuddling between him and the blanket for warmth. But for me, the depth of human degradation was touched when he told of the nightly queues of men four deep waiting to go into a brothel.

Ten days of leave can be exquisite torture. Every hour is an hour less, every tick of the clock a moment nearer the inexorable return. After the first sixteen months, leave came at regular intervals of a year. Twice I accompanied him to London and saw him off on the troop train. To one who has walked in that silent throng of burdened men with rifles pointing up over their shoulders, returning from leave to the Front, there's no forgetting what war looks like.

He came back at the end with ravaged health, but whole in limb. And then we began to look for the new era that was to emerge from all the chaos of war. At first there was a great weariness, a horrible feeling of the morning after an orgy of bestiality: the sorry world seemed to be licking its sores. Then we saw the prolongation of the Blockade, involving the death of all Austrian children under the age of seven — a more thorough-going slaughter of the innocents than Herod's. There was the deliberate humiliation of a defeated enemy and the imposition of a fantastic war indemnity designed to enslave German working men and women for generations. As well as to make the world safe for democracy, the war was fought to put an end to military domination. It is not easy to conceive of a militarism more dominant than the one that drew up and imposed the Versailles Treaty. There was no mistaking the writing on the wall. I said to my husband: "If it all started over again and they wanted you, would you go?" And he replied: "They're not having me any more."

That's how I became a pacifist: by an irrefutable process of experience. They told us it was a war to end war, and like simpletons we believed them. It was the bitterness of having been grotesquely swindled that struck deepest. What we had gone through didn't matter; but the certainty that it had all been in vain, that the millions of dead had been tricked into a futile sacrifice, ate like acid into the belief in war as a remedy.

We were left with the sure knowledge that whatever might set the world right, it was definitely not war.

Jessie Wood

Chapter Two: Reviews of *A Personal Record*

Introduction

D.H. Lawrence: A Personal Record was finally published by Jonathan Cape in May 1935. It received generally favourable reviews; Jessie was particularly appreciative of that in the *Times Literary Supplement*. (see Letter Three)

The only mention in the Nottingham press came in a reader's article in the *Nottingham Journal*, from which extracts are printed here.

Nottingham Journal, Wednesday 6th May 1935

What Our Readers Think
Two recent books on D.H. Lawrence

Sir — During the Jubilee days I have read two books about the personality of D.H. Lawrence, the most informing and illustrative of his character and temperament of any of the long series of books written about him. The one written by his wife contains new letters showing his turbulent spirit and constant necessity for a change of scene.

As a book it is not a success for the writer has not the slightest idea of style or cohesion of narrative, but simply like the other lady lover Lawrence called the Brett puts down what occurs to her mind at the moment. It is noticeable that here as well as in the book of the Brett that no two women lovers of Lawrence have ever been able to abide with each other.

The short book by E.T., the Miriam of *Sons and Lovers*, is the best of all those written about Lawrence, because from no other source can we discover how his character was made. In contrast to most of the others it is well written and not in haste. For the years of the life of Lawrence beginning with college, at Nottingham, and ending with *Sons and Lovers* the writer is almost Boswellian in the detail and intensity of her narrative. We know all about her own and the Lawrence family, her and his combined studies, their religious connections, his methods of study, his favourite books and characters of books.

If he had married E.T. she would have helped him to preserve a balanced literary judgement. His German wife cared nothing for literary judgement, but only wanted him for herself. To students of the character and personality of Lawrence only two books are now necessary, this personal record by E.T. and the large volume of collected letters edited by Aldous Huxley, in which volumes everything of importance will be found.

William Lewin
Wesley Cottage, Cotgrave

The Times Literary Supplement, Thursday May 9 1935

D.H. Lawrence and "Miriam"
D.H. Lawrence: A Personal Record. By E.T. (Cape 5s)

Among the many reminiscences of D.H. Lawrence put into print since his death, there has been at least no volume more truly vital than this unpretentious record set down by the woman who figured as "Miriam" in the autobiographical *Sons and Lovers*. Its virtue springs from two sources. In the first place, it is admirably written, combining sensitive feeling with candour and directness of statement. The passing of the years — a quarter of a century — has brought serenity without dulling the keen edge of either sorrow or joy. There is an immediacy in these re-presentations of youthful friendship and love, walks and talks, enthusiasms and quarrels, pain and gladness, which brings clear to the vision the living reality of what the young Lawrence was to this girl, and what she was and might in happier circumstances have been to him.

But there is more in it than that, more even than the fact of her having been his most constant chosen companion during his formative years from fifteen to twenty-five or so. *Sons and Lovers* still remains for many readers his most successful novel, and one which not only marks in itself a parting of the ways but depicts the actual psychological situation making it inevitable that he should take the path leading from rather than towards common human normality. In that situation his relation to the girl who was "Miriam" was plainly pivotal. As he presented the case it was that "Miriam" put to the test, had failed him. She gave him spiritual and intellectual, but shrank from passionate, fulfilment. Perceptive critics have more than once suspected a falsity, a one-sidedness, in this account: how truly, E.T.'s story now comes to show. It is an unhappy history, of boy-and-girl friendship, born of common interest in books and ideas, a friendship which seemed surely ripening to mutual love, disrupted suddenly by outside interference, so that "the issue of love in its crudest sense had been forced upon us while we were still immature and unprepared." Lawrence himself afterwards called it "the slaughter of the foetus in the womb." He, in his own words, "looked into his heart" and could not find that he loved her as a husband should, and thereafter never ceased for long to harp upon the impossibility of their marrying. They would continue friends but, he insisted, passion he must seek elsewhere; the two kinds of love, spiritual and sensual, were absolutely discrete. The attitude was probably inescapable for him in his psychological dilemma, bound to his living mother as he then was; but it is plain that he was at this time at the crisis of that inner division he later sought to evade by denying the intellect, though he then claimed to "trust entirely" to it. It is easy in the light of fuller knowledge to dismiss his family's interference as but the effect of an already deep and ineradicable cause, but can one be so sure? E.T.'s account convinces one that their affection was a natural, spontaneous growth out of which he might have won that liberation he never was to know. As it was he brought increasing unhappiness to them both, until "the shock" of his version of their story in *Sons and Lovers*, which she had urged him to rewrite with absolute truthfulness from an earlier, paler writing, "gave the death-blow to our friendship." She did not see him again after 1912.

This intensely personal and intimate history is throughout the centre of E.T.'s narrative, and rightly so from its crucial nature in Lawrence's development. But she has, incidentally, much else to tell, and of happier kind — her own home life at the "Willey Farm" of *Sons and Lovers*, and Lawrence's unclouded visits to the family there; excursions together about the countryside or to the sea; student encounters and discussions. There is one long and particularly interesting chapter on his early reading perhaps over ten years, a development from Rider Haggard and Anthony Hope to Whitman and Dostoevsky. She has to tell, too, of his first writings, printed and unprinted, of original and vanished versions of *The White Peacock* and *Sons and Lovers*, of how she brought about the first printing of his poems. There are accounts, too, of her visits to Lawrence's home, where she was always aware of an oppressive emotional intensity all too often directed against herself. There are some not unattractive glimpses of Lawrence's father, and of his mother a fuller portrait, less sympathetic but extremely living. Lawrence himself is drawn as a vivid, alert figure, in earlier days always gay and charming, but growing into ever more preponderant distress as his inner problems became more oppressive.

It was E.T.'s fortune to know his tenderness, "the inspiration of his gay and dauntless spirit." It was her lot, too, to experience that arrogance in him which, as she says, was a mask for his lack of conviction and wretchedness. She records both the happiness and the suffering he brought her with self-detachment and with insight into their significance for his being and future. It was inevitable that she should see his turning from her, and even more the manner of his turning from her, as his own first step upon the road which was to lead to "his own final despair." But in that assumption others will concur, and it is that fact which gives this book, apart from its obvious merits, its ultimate significance.

The Times, Tuesday May 14, 1935

D.H. Lawrence as a Young Man
D.H. Lawrence: A Personal Record By E.T. (Cape 5s.)

The accounts of D.H. Lawrence published by his sometime friends and intimates have been of widely varying interest and literary merit. In either aspect the present small volume appears as one of the very best of them all. The writer has a genuinely important story to tell, and narrates it briefly and well. She writes frankly of her subject's charm and genius, and no less plainly of their painful differences and final divergence, but always with balance and an insight able to assess the deeper than personal issues.

These are extremely valuable, indeed vital, qualities in one whose fortune it was to be more closely and sympathetically associated with D.H. Lawrence as youth and young man than any other person, a relationship he acknowledged, though not without some distortion, in drawing the portrait of Miriam in the novel *Sons and Lovers*. She knew him first as fellow-pupil at Sunday school, then as visitor with his mother to her parents' farm, and so presently as confidant, comrade, and in some sense lover. From the age of 16 or less they discussed together problems of religion and life they could mention to no one else, they read the same books, and all his earliest writings were shown first to her. She brought about, in fact, the first publication of his poems in the *English Review*. "You," he once wrote to her, "the anvil on which I have hammered myself out," and the metaphor seems apt.

For she had, before all was done, to bear the brunt of no small part of the shaping of his metal. The placidity of their affectionate friendship was shattered by the demand coming from his mother that they should be formally "engaged" or else less intimate. They were not ready for the full issue of love thus thrust upon them, and the consequence was disaster. It need not have been so perhaps in most normal cases, but Lawrence, as E.T. early realized, was never normal. He was plunged into the maelstrom of emotional distresses reflected, but not fully narrated, in *Sons and Lovers*. They were irrevocably estranged during, and by, its writing, which she felt, not without ponderable cause, to be a betrayal of his integrity — and of her.

The story is well worth reading for its account of the younger Lawrence amid his family and friends, of his reading and development, of the writer's own home life. But also it is deeply illuminative of what Lawrence was then and what he was to become.

Daily Herald Review

Books of the week, Thursday May 16th 1935
Edited by Roger Pippett

Yet another contribution to the most lively literary controversy of recent years appears in *D.H. Lawrence: A Personal Record*, by E.T. (Cape 5s)

Its author, a Midland farmer's daughter, was the closest companion of the dead writer's youth. She met him first as a fellow-pupil at the local Sunday School. He visited her at her home, and soon they were walking through the woods and discussing everything under the sun, but mainly D.H. Lawrence.

She helped to get his earliest poems published, and he drew her portrait, after his fashion, as Miriam in *Sons and Lovers*, which remains, in many ways, his most sensitive and satisfying novel. And then he stormed out of her life as abruptly as he had stormed into it…

She has written a quiet, frank, sensible and most revealing study of one of the queerest — and most significant — fishes that ever swam in the cold, green sea of English literature.

And she has done her work so well that we not only see the young shy-proud Lawrence, but we can also glimpse the man and the artist he was to be.

The Sphere June 8, 1935

The World of Books
Reviewed by VERNON FANE

The fundamental character of what is probably D.H. Lawrence's best novel, *Sons and Lovers*, has always seemed to me to be Miriam. The internal conflicts of Paul Morel and his relationship with Miriam, blocked by that mother-love, are delineated with the clarity of Lawrence's personal experience. As "E.T." says in *D.H. Lawrence: A Personal Record* (Cape 5s), the novel was written "under the influence of something amounting to a frenzy."

But the character of Miriam always remained vague and unreal, as though she were the *bel sans merci* herself. I had always, perhaps not consciously, suspected that Lawrence had purposely (if an action carried out in a time of emotional frenzy can be called purposeful) kept the character of Miriam unreal, had distorted it in order to comfort and convince himself, and had kept it vague in order that there should be no doubt about the laurels of victory which, at the cost of so much suffering to himself, he was to place upon his mother's head.

It is pleasant to have this suspicion confirmed by "E.T.", the original of Miriam, who says: "He had to present a distorted picture of our association so that the martyr's halo might sit becomingly on his mother's brow. But to give a recognizable picture of our friendship which yet completely left out the years of devotion to the development of his genius — devotion that had been pure joy — seemed to me like presenting *Hamlet* without the Prince of Denmark... Neither could I feel that he had represented in any degree faithfully the nature and quality of our desperate search for a right relationship... it was a subtle distortion of what had been the deepest values of my life."

The value of "E.T."'s book is that it corrects that distortion by filling in the character of Miriam, and it is well worth it if only to compare the two accounts of the emotional climax of *Sons and Lovers*, the scene by the haystack where Paul tells Miriam that their relationship cannot continue on the old footing.

But there is a good deal more than this — of Lawrence's youth and the influences which moulded his character — so much, in fact, that the book's only defect is its diffuseness.

The Yorkshire Post, **Wednesday June 19th, 1935**

D.H. Lawrence: A Personal Record By E.T. (Cape 5s)

"E.T." is the original of Miriam in *Sons and Lovers*. But it is easy to believe that the account there of her relationship with Lawrence is, as she says, by no means accurate. Lawrence, after all, was writing a novel, not a record of facts, and he often put distorted portraits into his stories. "E.T." however, is not concerned to defend herself: her book is agreeably free s. She tells us simply what Lawrence was like in his adolescence and early manhood, before his marriage, when she probably knew him better than anyone else.

Some points that emerge are the remarkable range of Lawrence's early reading; his intimate familiarity with nature and the English countryside — "There seemed no flower nor even weed whose name and qualities he did not know"; his irresistible charm as a companion and his cruelty as a friend; and the dominating position of Mrs Lawrence in the Lawrence household. More than most of the many books written about Lawrence, this short and unpretentious volume justifies itself by covering a period in Lawrence's biography hitherto left largely blank, and by revealing in the unknown youth many of the qualities later intensified in the famous man.

Chapter Three: Correspondence with May Holbrook

Introduction

Jessie had a close and loving relationship with her elder sister May, in whom she confided — rather than her parents — and relied on for advice, particularly during the time her relationship with Lawrence was ending.

Two series from their correspondence survive: twelve postcards and one letter which are previously unpublished, sent by Jessie between 1907 and 1913 from excursions and holidays; and three letters sent to May (by now well established in Canada) in 1930 and 1935 which were previously published in Nehls' *D.H. Lawrence: A Composite Biography*. This is certainly not the full extent of their correspondence, but it has not been possible to trace any other surviving examples.

Postcards

[Undated]

We have not long since returned from Whitby where we have had a most delightful day. We walked there and arrived home by train. It is a queer quaint old town with beautiful views of the old abbey. Rigg Mill we have not yet visited but hope to have an excursion there shortly.
I hope mother is improved. We are having a splendid time.

J

Comment

This card was undated and unaddressed but we know it was sent from a holiday with the Lawrence family at Robin Hood's Bay — the second time Jessie had accompanied them on their summer vacation — and therefore it can be dated August 1907. (*A Personal Record* pp. 126-8)

May had married Will Holbrook the previous November but was still living at the Haggs with her parents. The trip to Rigg Mill was made before 20th August, when Lawrence wrote to Gertrude Cooper (*Letters vol 1* p. 36).

9 August 1910, Mrs W Holbrook, Moorgreen

I suppose you have returned home by now! Did you have a good time at Arno?

We went to Spurn yesterday. We had a very good time, it is delightful there, like a little island all to oneself, just such a spot as you dream of sometimes, where you may lie on the sand with the sea at your feet, and watch the vessels sail lazily round the horizon. That is all you wish for; it is life enough. I would like to be there today.

J

Love to Will

Comment

The card was posted in Grimsby so possibly Jessie was staying on the Lincolnshire coast where she had enjoyed an earlier holiday in Mablethorpe with the Lawrences. The identity of her companion is not known.

21 April 1911, Mrs W Holbrook, The Cottage, Moorgreen

I have looked everywhere for a card that does justice to this magnificent old park [Knole], and this is the best I can find.

It is very fine and large, the trees suggest the pillars of a cathedral.

We want to stay the night and are looking for a room. I come home on Sunday.

J

Comment

This card and the two following were sent from excursions and holidays with Helen Corke.

16 August 1911, Mrs W Holbrook, The Cottage, Moorgreen
From the King's Writing Closet, Hampton Court.

Greetings: We are spending a day in this lovely old palace, walking beneath avenues of lime beside long reaches of water paved with the placid broad leaves of water lilies. I could hardly decide which view to send, you would like so many.

J

We go to Plymouth tomorrow (by rail)

1 August 1912, Mrs W Holbrook, The Cottage, Moorgreen

We are in Cologne this afternoon (Wednesday). Have been in the cathedral which is more lovely than I can say. It is Catholic: people are continually coming in to pray before images, candles are burning and there is a smell of incense.

Sailing down the Rhine is very jolly. The boat is most comfortable. This morning we had an hour in Dusseldorf. Yesterday we had tea (coffee rather) in Emmerich, a quaint little town a day's journey down the river. We are having a good time.

Love to Will

Jessie

Comment

Helen Corke did not share Jessie's enthusiasm for the holiday. She felt alone, with Jessie seeming detached and spending much time reading *The Brothers Karamazov*. (*In Our Infancy* p. 220)

6 July 1913, Mrs Holbrook, Wolds Way, Plumtree

La Sainte Chapelle is the most beautiful sight I have seen in Paris. Fill this picture with the most gorgeous blues, reds and purples and you have some idea of the marvellousness of this jewel of form and colour.

The Blue Review is dead. There is no August number.

If they do not return my MS soon I must write them.

I am going about all alone, it is jolly.

J

Comment

The Holbrooks had moved from Moorgreen to Plumtree after May was given a teaching job in Keyworth. This card and all the following relate to Jessie's visit to France to stay with her pen-friend Marc Boutrit. *The Blue Review* was a magazine edited by Middleton Murry and Katherine Mansfield. Jessie's manuscript was possibly of her novel *The Rathe Primrose* which has not survived.

4 August 1913

I send this as being appropriate in case you have had no rain yet.

Today we have been to Notre Dame. I climbed to the top of the tower — an immense height. The city is beautiful — the river winds in and about — from that tower I counted 8 bridges from one side only.

Yesterday we went to see the Great Water at Versailles — that is, the fountain all playing — a beautiful sight. I write from the Bois de Boulogne. Mrs C, an active lady of 60 or so, takes me about.

You'd laugh to see us sat outside a cafe and drink a glass of bock. Give my love to Will.

J

14 August 1913, Thursday from St Genis

Thank you very much for the *Westminster*. It is for the Dostoevsky review you have sent it chiefly isn't it? It is very good — I have always thought Dostoevsky greater than Tolstoi but it seemed sacrilege to say so.

You will have had my letter by today, I expect. It is very jolly here — you would like it.

Love to Will

J

Comment

This and all following cards were sent when Jessie was staying at St Genis, the home of Marc Boutrit. The town is in south-west France in the province of Bordeaux.

28 August 1913

Many thanks for your letter. I try to remember your good advice, having before me the shining lights of my various ancestors, but when it comes to *eau-de-vie* of 1864 the temptation is great, you'll admit. I must confess to a preference for *eau-de-vie* above other liqueurs (I am forgetting how to spell).

Certainly I will write a heart to heart epistle, but considering I opened that organ to the extent of 5 pages in a letter to Pawny yesterday perhaps it is advisable to close it for a space lest the escape be too rapid.

One thing I always remember — Plumtree is a haven in England which is the home country.

Love

J

Comment

Pawny was the nickname of Jessie's grandfather Jonathon, a pawnbroker who died in 1890. The reference is possibly to a cousin, another Jonathon who in 1911 was a wine merchant's traveller with a daughter named Jessie.

8 September 1913, La Rochelle, Monday

We have spent a delightful day here Marc and I on our way to La Vendée where we shall stay at Fernando's house until Thursday probably. La Rochelle is very old and very interesting.

Thanks much for the *Westminster*. I shall be glad when I hear again from you or Will. My time here is drawing to a close.

Love

J

Comment

La Vendée is a *département* on the Atlantic coast. The identity of Fernando is not known. *The Westminster Gazette* published short stories by Lawrence in the issues of 6th and 13th September. (*Letters* Vol II p. 67)

11 September 1913

We are by the seaside again facing the full Atlantic. I have bathed — the sea was very strong, the wind a little cold, but I feel a fine glow in my skin.

I have just helped Marc to write your card while the vilest mechanical piano shrieked a dance tune. This coif belongs to Vendée and is the cap worn by the old lady where I am staying. We have fine interesting times.

What heaps I shall have to talk about all winter!

Love to Will

J

Friday 18 September 1913, St Genis

Thanks much for your letter and enclosed cuttings. I like especially the crit. of Gertrude Bone's *Women of the Country*.

I think you must not attempt to cash my cheque — you will commit forgery if you sign it for me. It will be valid until after October. I am at present not quite spent up.

I am coming home on Monday — travelling all Monday night, I hope to arrive in Nottm by 3.30pm on Tuesday. I have told mother to meet me. Should like well to come to the Park — but I'm sure mother will like me to go right home first. Was at Bordeaux yesterday — have bought you a *Cafetière Russe* — you'll have lovely coffee henceforth.

Until a few days

J

Sunday night June 1913, 22 Ella Road, West Bridgford

Dear May, I have just returned from seeing Nell off. We had a fine walk to the trams and got home by five to a glowing fire. Then after a leisurely tea we set out for Victoria.

I think we did well not to come to Lincoln and stay with you instead. I think I shall look upon this weekend as unique — there seemed to be perfect harmony — a rare state and quite of the nature of things. It came of itself like a beautiful sunset, like a gift from the innate goodness of things. I feel as if one cannot be grateful enough for such a halt on the journey; it is so unattainable by mere outward means and it throws its radiance for so far over one's life. In years to come I am sure I will look back to this weekend with gladness and confidence — like to a beauty spot on a rather uphill road.

I wish if I could in any way, you would let me make up to you a little for being with you — I shouldn't offer, only that I know you are bound to miss Miss Philip's money. If you want anything from town, do let me get it for you.

I find I have left my tooth brush. I should be glad if you would send it on; you'll know it — a large white one.

Love to Will

J

I enclose Agnes Gregory's wedding card — it was waiting for me here.

Comment

In May 1913 Jessie wrote to Helen Corke about their planned visit to Lincoln, which was obviously aborted. Miss Philip was possibly a lodger with May. Agnes Gregory was married in April 1913. Her home was on Wellington Terrace in Eastwood. There is no other mention of her, but she was probably a schoolmate of the Chambers.

43 Breck Hill Road, Woodthorpe, Nottingham. March 10th 1930
[To May Chambers Holbrook, Cuffley, Sask., Canada]

My dear May,

I hope this letter will not be a shock to you; perhaps you have seen of Bert's death in your papers. I can only enclose cuttings, and cannot tell you any details because I never resumed correspondence with him. I had no idea he was ill, so it was a great shock to learn that he was dead.

I should very much like to be able to talk to you about things. Did you ever write to him from Canada, and did you ever hear from him? I think he has had a very strange and stormy life; to my mind he has made no development. I think he has been afraid to face the real problems of his own personality, but I am sure he has suffered terribly, and endured awful loneliness.

I feel terribly grieved when I think of what he has suffered, but I do not feel that I could have helped him. During all these years I have never regretted returning that letter to him — you remember it? It was the first after a year of silence; I showed it to you, and you said: "Send it him back, send it him back". Which I did because I felt it necessary to make a clean break. Yet, when I remember how he used to tell me, almost in despair, that, as an artist, he could not do without me, my heart aches, and I wonder if I did wrong. It can make no difference now, of course, but I never really felt hard-hearted towards him, and it was hard, indeed, to be parted from him. You understood best of anyone in those days, and I want to thank you for all your unspoken kindness that helped me so much during that first terrible winter.

These last months I have felt such a desire to write to him, particularly when there was all the trouble about his pictures. Did you read of it? I felt he was Ishmael, with his hand against every man, and every man's hand against him, and I just wanted to tell him that I thought of him still with the old affection. But I did not write, partly because my operation came on just about that time. I feel sure, in my own heart, that all the fuss with the authorities over his pictures & his poems, has killed him. No doubt he was deeply mistaken about life, poor chap. Now I learn that David wrote to him a year ago, and have seen his reply, and how much his old self that was, but such yearning. If I had known of that, I could not have kept from writing. But they never told me until now.

I am going to ask you, my dear May, if you will send me back two books I once sent you. Never mind what condition they may be in; it doesn't matter, I should just like to have them for old times sake. They are (1) *The Golden Treasury of Songs & Lyrics*, in a *green* binding, and full of pencil marks. Bert gave me that little book for my birthday when I was nineteen; he dropped it into my hands when we [were] in the wood all among the anemones. I sent it to you at a time when I felt I must part with everything that could remind me of him, and indeed I have nothing left. So if you will let me have it back I shall be glad. The second one is a little collection of Browning's poems I sent to you. A little red book, I think. That we had read together many times, and I have never been able to find that particular edition in the shops. Do you know the two books I mean? If they are still in existence, do let me have them. To send you that *Golden Treasury* was like sending you my own heart, but it had to be done.

Now in return, please tell me some book you would like to have, and I will get it for you.

Don't let this grieve you; it is all so long ago — but some things last while life lasts. I cannot understand why feeling should be so deep and so constant, can you?

I shall trust you not to let anyone see this, not even Will, because it just reveals a little of what never has been revealed. But Death is a great and august event, and feeling, for once, may be forgiven. I think he had reached a terrible "impasse" in life, where he could go neither forward nor back; I was so afraid he might lose his reason, which would have been so much worse than death. Let us hope he has found the peace he never found on earth.

With love to you,

J.

I never saw him after that Sunday father & I drove over to your cottage & he returned with us as far as Watnall.

Comment

Jessie re-affirms her gratitude for May's guidance and support during 'that terrible winter' when her relationship with Lawrence ended.

Her request for the return of the *Golden Treasury* is a touching reminder of her feelings of 'the old affection' and her need for some memento of the good times shared with Lawrence.

The operation she mentions may have been on her leg, the recovery from which she reports to Helen Corke in March 1930 (*Collected Letters 20*)

43 Breck Hill Road /Woodthorpe /Nottingham /July 6th, 1930
[To May Chambers Holbrook, Cuffley, Sask., Canada]

Dear May,

I'm rather late in answering your letter. I found it waiting at the end of the Whitsuntide holiday, when we returned from a few days in London. I couldn't reply quickly because I was busy doing some writing which I will tell you about some day. Just yet I cannot say much, but when I can tell the whole tale, you shall hear it. You will be interested.

I am very glad you are sure now that I am truly alive. It is so indeed. When you went away, the time was still young; I have fought many a hard fight since then, but I have kept really alive with no veneer. Of course, one must have a face, 'to face the world with,' but that also is a true part of me, and I was always an excellent hand at keeping my own counsel.

Thank you for the enclosure. I shall keep it on account of the passages you have underlined. How very revealing they are! Poor chap — he must often have cursed himself for a "flat," as he used to say. It was precisely because he was naturally good that it all happened. But he has paid the price, to the uttermost farthing, and for that I honour him; it tells me that I was not mistaken when I looked at him and felt that he was a living manifestation of God. What I saw in him I can never tell to any human being, and you are one of the very few to whom I would try. But I was right, he was as great as I thought; I shall prove it to you later on. The trouble with him has been, that as a youth, the ideal of goodness that was rammed down his throat was a thoroughly rotten one. He submitted to it, knowing no better, and after he found out his mistake, he spent the whole of his strength in tearing it to pieces, like a tiger rending his prey. This has hardly been discernible yet, but it will be seen, and then he will take his place among the great — perhaps not the great artists, but among the great benefactors to mankind.

I remember well, when I put the anemones on the grave, you said, "It isn't finished; it's only just started." You were the best friend to me; you were always sympathetic, and you asked no questions, — how great a boon that was, you can never know. If you had tried tiresomely to 'understand', it would have been fatal. So once more I thank you for your help and real 'understanding'.

I like the article you sent; it is in the book of *Assorted Articles*. In a while I'll send this book for you to read; and then perhaps you will post it back to me — it costs 6/— which is more than it is worth (of our money).

I must disagree with you when you say that inspiration is off its pedestal. It is rather the other way about. The greatest scientists of today admit that science can only go so far, and that the kind of truth that true inspiration teaches is beyond the reach of science. That is true of Einstein and all the great figures in the scientific world of today.

Speaking on my own little account I must tell you in all seriousness and sincerity that, but for divine help, I could not have come through unmaimed. For I was really stricken unto death, and I had to fight for my life, but in very truth help came to me that I can only call divine. I am sure that it is so — it must have been so with the saints of old, those who died and suffered for a faith. And you know, no faith is the true faith, because faith itself enlarges according to our vision, and thus changes from age to age.

What do you think of *The New Adelphi*? You like the Portrait, don't you? Of all the articles I think Bert's own is far and away the best. How well he remembered the old places! In my opinion, had he but had the physical strength to live, we might have witnessed something in the nature of a miracle. But we are all too unbelieving for such things to happen, and it is hard to see aright.

How are things going with you? Here it is a perfect, fresh Sunday morning. I did the cooking yesterday, so am free to write today. What are your crops looking like? How I wish you could get a bumper year, and sport a holiday.

Did you get a dress length recently? Did you care for it?

We are hoping to go abroad this year, to Slovenia — Ljubljana is the town we are making for, if it comes off. Will tell you more later.

With love to you and Will
(By the way, does Will need more powder?)
Jessie.

Comment

The New Adelphi produced a special DHL edition in 1930 which contained a photo taken in Mallorca the previous year and Lawrence's essay on *Nottingham and the Mining Countryside*.

43 Breck Hill Road, Woodthorpe, Nottingham. June 21st, 1935
[To May Chambers Holbrook, Cuffley, Sask., Canada]

My dear May,

I was very glad to get your letter of a week or two ago. It seemed such a long time since I had heard from you. Now you are in the midst of the busy season, and I hope things are promising well. By the way it was not your parcel that I thought was 'a bit of a fluke', but the one I sent to Will, containing old socks & tobacco.

Now to leave Keyworth news and come to some of my own. I told you some time ago that a young Frenchman, Emile Delavenay, had applied to me for information about Bert, on whom he is writing a most exhaustive thesis. I supplied him with notes as to our reading and so on. Later on Professor Lavrin happened to see these notes, and begged me to let him publish them in a magazine he was bringing out called *The European Quarterly*. Then Jack suggested I should make a book of my notes etc. He pointed out that I was giving away this information to others who were making use of it, and that I might just as well publish it myself. So the long and short of it is that I have written a short book on our old friend, which has been published by Jonathan Cape. I am sending you a copy in a day or so. Perhaps you won't have time to read it in this busy season, but never mind, it will be there for when you have time. I think you will be interested in it, and I shall be delighted and anxious to know what you and Will think of it, and please tell me just what you *do* think. Remember there is no hurry; bide your time, and talk about it in a letter when you feel inclined. *You*, more than anyone, know what those years were to me, and you may guess what the writing of this book has meant, in joy and in sorrow. But I am very glad it is done. It is a great relief to mind and spirit. I felt, too, that I had a duty to discharge. I knew a chapter of Bert's inner history that no one else did or could know, and it happened to be a vital chapter, lacking a knowledge of which his critics and commentators went sadly astray.

I want you to realise that I can never forget your sympathy of those times, which was the more precious because it was nearly always unspoken. Nevertheless, I knew it was there, and it made all the difference. Your cottage was a haven in a world that had become almost wholly a desert. I don't think I need say any more. It goes deeper almost than words can go, but I have never once forgotten what it meant to me. So, as you shared in the joys and sorrows of those days, I want you to share a little of the fruits of them. Cape's have paid me £25 on account of royalties on the book. Whether there will be any more depends upon the sales, and I believe the book is doing pretty well. So in the course of a few days I shall send you an order for £10. and I hope you will enjoy it in the way that appeals to you most. But *do* enjoy it, buy yourself something you've always been wanting.

Now I want to make a request. Do you mind not mentioning anything about the book to mother, or even perhaps to Hubert & Bernard. I have not spoken of it to any of our people except David. There is no reason why father & mother should not know, but I think it would only waken old, unhappy memories, and I simply don't want to talk about it with them. That's all. You'll understand, I'm sure. I must hurry now to catch the post, and will send on the book and money order within the next few days.

Jack joins me in sending love to you both. I hope you are both well, and enjoying the summer.

Yours with love,

Jessie

Chapter Four: Two Sketches

These two drawings are the only known examples of Jessie's artwork. Very little information exists on their provenance.

Jessie commented on Lawrence's flower paintings in *A Personal Record* (p. 62) — perhaps a model for her 'Delphiniums' — but there is no mention of her own efforts in that account or her letters. 'Delphiniums' was on display in David Chambers' home in Wollaton — perhaps a gift from his sister? — until deposited in the University Manuscripts Collection by his daughter Ann.

A copy of the seascape was sent to Ann Howard in 1988 by her Canadian cousin Barney who stated that it was painted in 1920 — perhaps another sisterly gift, this time to brother Bernard. The original is still held in Canada. The location of the scene is not known.

Holiday scenes

These three views are from postcards sent by Jessie when on holiday (see Chapter 3). The first is Rigg Mill near Robin Hood's Bay where she accompanied the Lawrence family; the second a view of Knole Park visited with Helen Corke; and the third comes from a visit to the home of her French penfriend, Marc Boutrit.

Handwriting

Two examples of Jessie's script from postcards to her sister May.

Chapter Five: The Bankrupt

Introduction

In his account of the family history David Chambers refers to the suicide of his great-grandfather Thomas Newbold, who he believed took his life by drowning on account of the failure of his business in the lace trade, a tragedy that provided the basis for Jessie's story. The family were said to have been rescued from distress by colleagues and fellow businessmen. In particular, daughter Jane, who was to become the mother of Sarah Chambers, was taken in by the Morley family — one of the leading hosiery manufacturers in the city. But David had never heard what became of his great-grandmother Elizabeth*.

May Holbrook provided more detail in a series of letters to David, but there is no other mention of drowning as the cause of death.

Daughter Jane was "orphaned" at the age of three, which would date the suicide to around 1827 — Jane was baptised on 20 January 1824 at Nottingham St Mary, the fourth child of Thomas and Elizabeth. It would be more accurate to say she was rendered fatherless since it was most probably her mother Elizabeth who was buried at Radford in February 1835 at the age of fifty.

The parish register of Radford church includes an entry for the burial of Thomas Newbold of Radford, aged forty-five, on 5th of March 1826. On the 11th of that month the *Leicester Chronicle* included an account, originally in the *Nottingham Herald*, of the inquest on the body of Newbold, a twist lace hand of Hyson Green who had destroyed himself by cutting his throat with a razor. He left a wife and four small children. A verdict of insanity was recorded. It seems that to save his children further distress, they were led to believe he had drowned.

According to Helen Corke, Jessie's story was written in the autumn of 1910. She was not satisfied with her original drafts and asked for comments from Helen who suggested several revisions. The revised version was sent to Edward Garnett in 1912 who found it "full of fine quality and true feeling." George Zytaruk judged it to be "an impressive example of her own power as a creative writer." (*Collected Letters* p. xi)

*See Nehls: *D.H. Lawrence: A Composite Biography* p571

It was submitted to the *The English Review* but was not published until its inclusion in the Nehls biography.

Jessie gives a surprisingly modern understanding of the weight of expectation on a male breadwinner, but as the story begins and ends with the domestic setting, and the wife's concern for her husband and her children, we wonder what strength it will take for her to survive. Both her theme of the unnatural limits placed on us by a capitalist society and her writing about nature which shows a profound connection beyond mere description, link her to Lawrence. In nature the man's 'superficial' self seems to disappear, the river absorbs him as a 'conscious, majestic power'.

The Bankrupt
by Jessie Chambers Wood

A little girl sat in the glow of firelight singing. She clasped her doll tightly with small brown hands and rocked herself in a low rocking chair.

On the hearth rug another girl, ten years old, knelt, cutting out paper men to amuse a fat baby boy. He was not interested in paper men and stretched out his hands trying to catch hold of his mother's skirt as she passed to and fro, laying the table for tea.

"Do keep him quiet till I've finished. He's getting so heavy to carry about." The mother spoke wearily, keeping with an effort her tone free from irritation. She unloosed the baby's fingers, while the sister rapped the steel bar of the fender with a spoon. This pleased him; he seized the spoon and aimed weak blows at the fender: the spoon flew from his fingers and Matilda had to search for it.

"Look here, our John, it isn't fair. I've minded baby all afternoon, and you've done nothing but read," she said in an aggrieved tone, to a brother a year younger than herself. A volume of *Chatterbox* lay across his knees and he bent towards the firelight, reading eagerly.

"That's what girls are for; it's your work," he muttered without looking up.

"Well it isn't very fair. That's my book — you know it is," she answered, with tears in her voice.

The baby had tired of the music of the spoon and began to cry fretfully.

"Let's show him the pictures! Shall you?" Matilda asked pleadingly. The boy assented, laying the book on the rug; the girl brightened.

"Now, baby, look! Pretty pictures, oh-h pretty!" John turned over the pages while his sister held back the baby's struggling hands. To keep him interested and to preserve the book from damage was a difficult and exciting occupation: they became flushed and noisy. The child in the rocking chair sang on imperturbably: the mother, passing between kitchen and dining room, found herself moving to the rhythm of the little one's hymn.

It gave additional fluency to the easy motion of her body. She was pleasing to see as she came towards the firelight and its glow rested upon her white skin, and thick smooth fair hair. Her mouth was firmly set, and little shadows danced about it pencilling heavily the lines which childbirth had traced there. But for these one might have discounted her thirty-three years: yet she carried a sense of latent power which lived in every ordered movement.

Each time she went down the passage to the kitchen she glanced at the door of the back parlour which faced that of the dining room. It was closed; it had not been opened since early morning.

She paused before it in returning for the last time, the filled tea pot in her hand. The noise from the dining room deterred her: she passed on. "No, I'll put them to bed before I disturb him."

She called the children to the table. The boy and girl lifted the baby upon their joined hands, and so, with his arms about their necks and his fingers clinging in their hair, carried him noisily to his high seat. The little girl laid her doll in the rocking chair and tucked it round with a tiny shawl; then stood sucking the end of her finger and looking thoughtfully at the table.

"Come and sit down, Dorcas, there's a good girl."

"Where's Dadda?" she asked, not moving.

"Oh he'll come soon. See, I've poured out your tea."

"Let me fetch him. I want to. Can I?"

"No, dear, he's busy."

"I want him. Can I fetch him? He likes me to fetch him," she persisted, slowly backing towards the door.

"Oh, he's ever so busy. He didn't hear me when I knocked a little while ago."

"I don't want my tea." The child's voice shook, she reached blindly for the door handle. "I want to fetch Dadda. Can I?"

The baby had crammed his mouth too full: he was on the point of choking. While the mother attended to him Dorcas slipped from the room. She closed the dining room door and stood an instant staring along the dark passage, then she ran to the door of the back parlour and beat upon it with the palms of her hands.

"Dadda — Dadda — let me in," she called softly.

There was no answer. She waited a moment and battered the door afresh.

"Dadda. I want to tell you something — Dadda, let me in — it's Dorcas." She leaned her head on the door and listened eagerly, but heard nothing from within: she straightened herself and took a step backwards, glancing fearfully towards the deserted kitchen where a point of gas light like a strange little eye looked at her. Then she began again, beating and calling low, her voice growing thick with tears.

Presently a chair was pushed, as if someone moved it in rising, and she stood tense and quivering. Footsteps crossed the room and the door opened. She ran forward and hugged her father's knees. "Why didn't you let me come in, Dadda. I've been waiting ever such a long time."

He lifted her without speaking: she clung about his neck. He sat down in his chair by the table and set her on his knee, drawing her warm trembling little body close. So they sat a moment; then he began to realise the stiffness of his limbs, and rose slowly to pace about the room with her in his arms.

"Well, what did you want to tell me?"

She began running her fingers through his fine dark hair.

"Should I make you some curls, Dadda?"

"But I thought you had something to tell me," he persisted gently.

She pressed her face against his neck. "I didn't want my tea," she whispered.

"And you do now?"

"Um!" — with a nod — "if you come with me."

He sat down for a moment, still holding her tightly. His gaze wandered absently round the room. The open bureau and the table were littered with papers: more papers, which appeared to have been sorted and arranged, lay upon the seats of three leather-covered chairs.

"Well, then, must we go, Dorcas," he said wearily. She hugged him, laughing: he rose and carried her into the dining room.

"I didn't know it was tea time till Dorcas fetched me," he said apologetically to his wife as he set the child in her chair.

"I thought you didn't want to be disturbed; I had knocked once or twice."

"Yes, I've been very busy," he answered without looking at her.

The children were eating silently, gazing at him with grave curiosity. He felt he could not bear their scrutiny: it imposed upon him some demand that he might not meet. He drank a cup of tea and left the table with a muttered apology. The mother had devoted herself studiously to the baby's needs: the two had not exchanged a single glance.

After tea began the bustle of getting ready for bed. The mother sat by the fire on a low chair holding the baby; the children stood by, watching her deft untying of each little garment: ready to receive it as it was slipped off. They must play each in turn with the rosy bare limbs, kicking and waving in the firelight. While the mother spread the bath sheet and carried in the bath Matilda was in charge: she held the baby, naked but for his tiny vest, very carefully. She clasped him tightly round his soft little body, but he wriggled and squirmed to get down on the rug. The other children laughed, but Matilda was frightened, for without clothes there seemed to be no way of keeping hold of him, and the faster she hugged him the more did he struggle. At last she let him slide down before her, and knelt over him, playing with his hands and feet.

In the bath he was regal. Each child went up to be splashed, and retreated in mock terror, while the baby shouted and slapped the water till it hissed upon the hot iron of the grate.

They all undressed by the fire. When they were ready for bed Matilda led the way, carrying the candle. Dorcas crept behind and stopped at the door of her father's room. The mother missed her and turned round half way up the stairs, the baby in her arms.

An unusual anger flashed into her eyes at the sight of the child lingering by the door. "Dorcas!" she exclaimed. The child shrank at the strange harshness of tone. She followed the others upstairs and got quickly into bed.

The house was large, built at the time when the lace trade had been in its first flush of prosperity. With its decline and the need for an ever-narrowing economy the unnecessary rooms had been one by one divested of furniture till now but three bedrooms were in use. The empty rooms seemed sinister as if they harboured a spirit of loneliness that was secretly seeking to eject the inmates and claim for itself the whole. The mother hated the place, marked with so many tokens of lost things, and hated more to leave the children there: their room but a small oasis of light and warmth in a waste of desolation.

She glanced resentfully at the closed parlour door as she came downstairs. She emptied the water out of the bath and folded the bath sheet. When the children's clothes were put away she decided to lay supper.

She took the table cloth from the drawer, and stood with it a moment in her hand. She half unfolded it, then flung it down upon the table and went impetuously to the parlour, opening the door quietly and closing it with a steady hand. Within her husband sat beside the fire.

He shivered slightly as she entered and turned involuntarily from her, bending towards the grate, which was choked with the ashes of burnt papers. She knelt on the rug before him and put her hands on his shoulders.

"Why do you stay away from me? Can I do nothing but keep your house?" her voice vibrated with pain and resentment. He moved, stretching his muscles to control them.

"I'm sorry," he said. His throat felt closed: he fancied the words like air bubbles rising, unchosen. "I... What is it you want to know?"

"What do you think I want to know?" she retorted passionately. "There is only one thing I care about: you know it well enough. Why do you shut yourself up alone? Why can't I share your trouble? You are cruel — you are cruel and wrong!"

She leant against his knee: he could feel the long sobs she suppressed. He looked away: stared at the uncurtained window where the gas flame reflected. The soft dark blue of his eyes dilated and his forehead quivered. He sat still, one hand supporting his head, the other hanging loosely by his side. Soon she raised herself and became calm. She rose to her feet and spoke coldly.

"I'm very sorry I've troubled you. I ought to have known better, considering all things, Only I fancied that if something was hurting you I might be able to help."

She stood for a moment looking down at him. She trembled a little and could scarcely restrain herself from clasping him to her. But she set her mouth resolutely and turned to go.

He moved uncertainly, almost writhing, averting his face yet more.

"No — no — you're wrong, very wrong," he said, huskily.

She stopped and echoed him: "Wrong?"

He felt her eyes upon him: they seemed to burn him. He got up and walked across the room as if to escape. The bitterness faded out of her eyes as she watched him: he was beautifully made, all supple and winsome. Her protective instinct asserted itself suddenly: for the moment there seemed but little difference between the man and the baby, only the man was infinitely more pathetic. He faced her and her eyes hardened as he avoided a direct gaze.

"Well, perhaps I only pain you. You would rather I did not know," she said, evenly, and moved towards the door.

"Don't go," he said. She waited, near the door; he walked to the table and stood leaning over it, his eyes fixed upon the litter of papers.

"What is there I can tell you? I don't know myself." He moistened his lips and forced out the words.

"No?" she said, gently and encouragingly. He winced and threw himself again into his chair.

"You see I've never looked far enough ahead —" She waited, but he did not continue.

"Well, don't worry. We shall manage to get along all right," she said sympathetically. The ready and tactless optimism stung him. She started at his harsh laughter.

"There — now I can tell you. No, we've done getting along; there's no more road for us: we've done, altogether."

"What do you mean?" she asked sharply, watching him with anxiety. Her change of tone braced him; he went on more calmly.

"You know there's to be a meeting of the creditors?" He paused, watching her; she nodded.

"I've been trying to straighten things out — and they're worse — even — than I thought." He stopped and dared her eyes — she answered his gaze steadily.

'I'm a bankrupt," he said simply. She started: her eyes filled with tears. "No, look what you've got to realise upon. There are all the machines — and the warehouses," she cried eagerly.

He shook his head a little impatiently. "The machines will fetch the price of scrap iron," he said bitterly. "No," as she began to protest, "they've been valued."

"But they're in working order," she cried breathlessly.

"You know they can't compete with the new ones," he said.

"What of the combine that was going to keep new ones out. You joined that?"

"Ay — useless — foolish. The men who have brought in the machines could buy out the combine."

"Well, if your machines are obsolete there'll be other people bankrupt too," she said.

"Ay — there's Packer and Goode. They can't be fixed much better than I am. But it's different for them —" His voice dropped, the last words were barely audible.

"Why?" She looked at him in great distress. He did not answer, and she repeated the query.

"They'll go under and come out again." The words came with difficulty.

"Well, and so will you!" Her voice rang sharply, slightly touched with scorn at his easy acceptance of defeat.

"Ay!" he said, and was silent. His long hands twitched convulsively. His eyes were dull now, and the looseness of utter weariness hung about every line of his face. The woman stood motionless: he seemed to have cast a momentary spell upon her; she felt baffled as if she were groping in fog. She had to rouse herself to throw it off. She stood up and went to the fireplace: taking up the tongs she carefully placed the half-burnt pieces of coal in a little heap over the dull embers. The slight occupation brought relief: the absolute hopelessness vanished. She felt in touch once more with familiar things.

Her husband watched her deliberate building of the fire: the calmness of her movements fascinated him. Some great change had taken effect between them: he realised dimly that it had been long working unrecognised. But now he watched her as if from another state of consciousness. Presently she put down the tongs and turned to him resolutely, taking his hands and pressing them tightly in her own.

"We must be brave. We won't admit failure: we must win through in the end." She spoke rapidly, with dogmatic assertiveness. She looked at his drooping head and unstrung face — she grew strong with the instinct of motherhood, and rich in possession. "You must not think about it any more alone. There's nothing disgraceful in bankruptcy. It's misfortune, that's all. We'll begin again: we'll go slowly: we'll work together."

Her eyes were bright and defiant. A little smile touched his face. It was so curious to hear her talking on, blundering and blundering. Yet she was so self-content and so very far away that it did not seem to matter. Better that she should not understand.

"We shall have to send the children away. Mother would have Matilda and John until the worst pull was over, at any rate. Baby's too little to send anywhere, and Dorcas hardly makes any difference."

She was deliberate again; he was fascinated as before, wondering at the immense essential difference between her and himself. He looked into her clear grey eyes and assented to what she said without having heard her words.

At last she noticed his abstraction.

"Well, we needn't stay here talking. I was just going to put supper on the table. You've had scarcely anything to eat all day." She waited anxiously for his reply, but none came. He passed his hand restlessly over his forehead. Her anxiety increased.

"Come, dear — come and have your supper." He rose and stretched himself and then stood upon the hearthrug with his back to the fire: his hands behind him.

"I'll go out a bit first, I think."

"But you ought to eat something." Then, as he made a movement of impatience: "Very well — perhaps you'll get an appetite if you go out awhile. But don't be long."

He went into the hall to get his coat and hat; she extinguished the lamp and returned to the dining room. As he pulled on his overcoat he heard a movement on the stairs behind him, and turning, saw Dorcas creeping down close to the baluster, holding her long nightgown above her bare feet.

"Why, Baby!" He picked her up quickly; she clung fast to him. Her feet were icy, he clasped them in one hand.

"I never said goodnight to you, Dadda — and — and I had nasty feelings beside."

"Did something hurt you, Dorcas — where?"

"No — not hurt," she shook her head vigorously. "Nasty feelings — close round me."

The mother came into the hall on hearing the child's voice. She opened her lips to chide, then paused with an intuitive alarm. Dorcas was shrinking from her, almost cowering in the father's arms. He carried her to the fire.

"Why, you ought to have been fast asleep long ago," he said soothingly.

"I wasn't sleepy." She blinked in the strong light: she stared vaguely about the room, then dropped her head again on his shoulder. The roughness of his overcoat surprised her, she sat up suddenly and looked at him. "Are you going out, Dadda?" she asked with a deep sob in her breath.

"Not far. Now let mother take you to bed."

But she clung to him more tightly than ever and began to cry softly, her shoulders heaving.

"Give her to me. I shall have her ill," the mother said, frightened. He tried to loosen her arms, but she clutched him, shaking. "I think I had a fancy, Dadda," she whispered hoarsely, imploring.

"NO, no, go to mother, like a good girl," he said very gently.

"NOW I'm going to be cross, Dorcas, if you don't come to me at once," the mother said firmly, adding: "Father is tired tonight." The child was cowed at the tone and turned obediently.

"Why, you're like an icicle. Yes, you'll be coughing all night now!" She drew the rocking chair nearer the fire and sat down, chafing the little one's feet.

"Don't be gone more than half an hour, Henry. It isn't good for you to wait so long between meals."

He stood an instant looking at them, pulling on his gloves the while. The child had closed her eyes and lay inert upon her mother's lap, the dark curls rumpled against her sleeve. His wife did not look up, but rocked gently and rubbed the child's limbs. When he turned and went she did not notice the soft closing of the door. She sat until Dorcas was warm and sleepy — till to all appearance sleep had come, then she rose to carry her upstairs. But Dorcas stirred, and opened eyes flooded with the unreasoning fear that comes between sleeping and waking. The mother was troubled: she watched thoughtfully, looking for symptoms of some childish sickness.

Presently she was able to lay her upon the couch: she covered her with a rug and began to set the supper.

The front door slammed: the man walked quickly down the hill, descending between the warehouses from the elevation of the Lace-Market into the river flats. When the town lights were all above him — not until then — there came to him the sound of the slamming door. It stayed with him as he walked, strangely persistent; neither repetition nor re-echo, but an unvarying continuous sense in the background of his consciousness, like the sense of moving looms to one who spends the half of a lifetime among them. At first it brought the memory of the exterior of the house, and impressed peculiarly the appearance of the cracks in the wood panelling of the door. He thought of Dorcas, hoping that the noise had not startled her. He turned his steps the while by long habit through an open meadow by the river side.

It was a breathless autumn night: the trees seemed to be listening for a sound too rare and fine for human ears: the heavy dew-soaked grass seemed weighted with an intense life of its own. The pungent scent of the rotting leaves was as arresting as a voice: these were the only things in the depths of the soft silent night that had a distinct articulation. He picked up a handful and inhaled their keen fragrance. They were the more intensely living, he thought, through the working of death. He walked slowly under the trees that bordered the path.

Gradually the sense of the slamming door lost its local significance, assuming one more intimate; becoming unified with the feeling of disintegration he had experienced earlier in the evening. It became the snapping of a bond between self and self. He felt an utter detachment from all that had grown about him since the time when between childhood and manhood he had put aside, at his father's bidding, the demands of the eternal child within him: submitting himself to the iron tradition of his house. He breathed the atmosphere of a night twenty years before, when in the same small business parlour where he had passed today, he learnt something of his fundamental weakness. He had entered the room vowing defiance to his father's will — clinging passionately to his ideal, a wider, freer life than that of the counting house and factory: a more generous aim than any permitted by the following of a business career. He had stood before his father seeing that ideal as it appeared in his father's eyes, seeing it shrink and wither and become of no account, feeling himself powerless to sustain it. He had forced himself to make the protests which had seemed so compelling, and had been abashed at their feebleness. And in the end he had yielded and bound himself to the gratification of his father's wish, and to the business fortunes of his family. Heaven and earth reeled in the revulsion that followed: in his self-abasement he could draw no relief but from the determination to make at least a success of his life upon its inevitable plane. He would put away all the visions of beauty for which he was not worthy.

He had straitly disciplined himself, striving to excel, painfully familiarizing himself with the minutiae of his trade, studying assiduously the movements of the industrial world. But always the progress of his affairs was checked by an unbalanced judgment and the actions of a spasmodic generosity. After the death of his father the prosperity of the house steadily declined.

Beyond the point where he now stood he could see nothing. He had no more faith in the virtue of his struggle: subconsciously he had realised the growing domination of the old self: it was rising, untrammelled, the stronger for its long repression. And while he was glad to feel it lifting, sweet and strong, he yet suffered an anguish of defeat, knowing that in face of the sure judgment of the world he had no intelligible plea to put forth. The bitterness of the past day had centred round this conviction.

He reached the path which followed the river, a little above its sloping green banks, and sat down upon the protruding roots of a great elm. A thin mist floated over the river; beneath the mist the water ran swiftly — a deep stream neglected of the city, for it gave nothing willingly, and brooked ill the harness of men. He listened to the whispering of innumerable eddies as they swirled softly away in the dark under the mist covering, and the quiet lapping of the water against the banks suggested to him the warm patting of a child's hands. Beyond the river the mist spread itself out over the marshes white and boundless, broken only by the shadowy forking of an isolated tree. There seemed to pass from him, as he sat, the last traces of the superficial self he had so hardly acquired — its pursuits, its standards, its interpretations; in the mist world before him was nothing more formless than they; scarcely more real appeared the surrounding of his physical existence. And though a lethargy woven of weariness and the spell of the river was upon his senses, there was yet an activity working tirelessly beneath them and by its agency he knew assuredly the dissolution of these things to be complete and final.

He rose suddenly, and moved nearer to the water: as he crossed the path the clock of St. Mary's struck nine. It was time to return home.

He stood still, trembling violently while throughout his dulled body there surged, like a cold wave seething, its dread of an essential, inevitable change. He stumbled towards the bank and leaned against a tree, faint and shuddering: gradually he slid downwards and lay in the grass. Before his brain, doors were swinging noiselessly, swinging backwards and forwards without reason or impetus.

Presently the shuddering ceased. "The door did slam," he said, and lay quiet.

Then through his stupor flowed the soothing of the river's voices: the current was swollen with heavy autumn rains, and the water slid past but a few inches below his head. When he opened his eyes he beheld the river: it absorbed him with its imperturbable flow, with the eternal measure of its irresistible motion. Its strength, its being, assumed gigantic proportions: it became a majestic, conscious power, filling the whole valley, lifting itself upwards and outwards to the hollowing of the night.

Supper was laid: Dorothy sat waiting her husband's return. She still felt uneasy about the child, and listened with some anxiety to her breathing. It was uneven, and the nostrils too worked rapidly. The eyelids were barely closed; between the upper and lower lids a tiny strip of the iris could be seen, and below the eyes were dark rings.

Dorothy bent down, putting her ear close to the lips, listening for the muffed sound heralding bronchitis. The child suddenly opened her eyes wide, and shivered with a terror of half waking. The mother shaded the light with her hand and stood motionless. In a little, Dorcas slept again. Dorothy glanced at the clock. The time was half past eight.

She went softly to her sewing table under a window in the corner of the room, and took from a drawer the twill frock she was making for the baby. She seated herself so that her shadow fell over the couch, and began to sew rapidly, absorbed in thought. She tried to see clearly the immediate future with its limitations and possibilities. She would have to part with the two elder children for a time, but for their welfare she was not concerned: her parents would take them gladly. The two younger ones cost little as yet. Henry, she knew, would never give up Dorcas, So, having roughly arranged the matter of the children, she turned to the consideration of her husband's position. This gave her more trouble.

She was not entirely ignorant of the ordinary course of circumstances following upon a man's bankruptcy. But it was difficult to imagine Henry in such a situation. She felt baffled with regard to him: she could not plan for him. Something in him puzzled her: she had never felt so foiled before: she hated the feeling of helplessness his attitude imposed upon her. As she thought of him she grew unquiet, sewing more and more rapidly, until her hands became unsteady, and she laid the work down almost from exhaustion. The clock struck ten. She turned in astonishment: she had not noticed the striking of nine. The table, set for two, was a mute interrogation. She folded up the little frock and went to the outer door, where she stood looking up and down the street.

About a hundred yards below the house, on the opposite side of the street, rose the tall straight outlines of her husband's factory. She looked intently at the windows of his room, and her heart leaped as she fancied she saw the glimmer of a light in one of them. She ran forward to make certain, and found the glimmer to be the reflection of a street lamp. She retraced her steps slowly and stood again in the bar of light which streamed through the open doorway.

She returned to the dining room on tiptoe, afraid lest Dorcas should be roused by her entrance. She felt a repugnance to the intensity expressed in the child's eyes, and to the terror that swept visibly through her newly awakened consciousness. But Dorcas slept, breathing unevenly still, as if she had sobbed herself to sleep.

For lack of any other occupation, Dorothy took up her sewing again. Presently her ear, keenly alert, registered the more regular breathing of the child, and after a while, seeing that the eyelids were completely fallen, and the little figure in deep repose, she decided that she might safely carry her to bed. When she came downstairs, she found it impossible to rest alone: the dining room with its generations of associations became articulate. Dorothy had never taken root in the old house. Its spirit was antagonistic, and she felt on sufferance with relation to it. Its furniture was not of her choosing, dating mostly from the time of the marriage of Henry's father. She had no real heritage, and in earlier days, before the birth of the children, fancied herself regarded as an intruder. Even now, her nerves being at a tension, the sideboard seemed frowning upon her, and all the silent furniture expressing an unalterable antipathy. The portraits of Henry's father and grandfather, reflected in the mirror above the mantelpiece, looked down austerely.

At eleven o'clock, steps came along the street. She sat erect and listened, holding her breath. They passed straight on, and as the sound of them died away far down the hill she found herself trembling.

She remembered the glimmer of light on the warehouse windows, and began to persuade herself that she had been mistaken in supposing it the reflection from a lamp. Perhaps, after all, he was only lingering about the place that had been his so long. The idea, once conceived, grew rapidly: she pictured him in the deserted rooms among the useless machinery, grieving for the consequences of his mismanagement. Suddenly impatient, she rose to go and find him, reproaching herself for not having done so sooner.

She fetched an old lantern, dusted it, fixed a candle in the worn socket, and, taking the emergency key, went out quietly, leaving the door ajar. She would not look again at the illumined window, but, fumbling, fitted the key into the great lock, setting the lantern on the ground and pressing with both hands to turn it. Then she pushed the door back slowly and went in. Her light seemed devoured by the darkness of the hall.

The warehouse had once been a family residence. From the entrance a flight of shallow stairs led to the rooms where the machines stood. She mounted, holding the lantern high to light the steps before her. At the top she paused and listened, but the heavy throbbing of her blood deafened her: she could not trust her hearing. She wanted to call his name, but she had not the courage, dreading the empty echo of her own voice.

The room was very long. One end from ceiling to wainscot was glassed: this great window gleamed grey in the dusk, its crosswork of frames standing high and black. There was a gangway leading from the doorway down the centre of the room, flanked on either side by the machines, each like an animal, crouching for the spring. Dorothy made an effort to control the beating of her heart, and forced herself to take long breaths. Then she walked slowly along the gangway, turning the light from side to side, fearing almost equally what she might or might not see. She reached the window: nothing had moved but the great shadows of the machines which sped silently behind at each turn of the lantern. It suddenly occurred to her that the machines were condemned and awaited destruction. A feeling of pity gave her courage: she looked with interest and commiseration over the grim iron outlines. They had dignity and purpose; the rigidity of their form belied their subtlety. She remembered the long quiet days succeeding the birth of each one of the children, when she had lain inert in a warm calm of existence, and the humming of the machines had woven into her drowsy soul. She grieved to think that they would spin no more.

As she went downstairs she knew she had not expected to find her husband in the factory. She hurried home, trying to believe that he had entered during her absence. His overcoat was not hanging in the hall.

The fire was low in the dining room. She put on coal, and sat down in the small rocking chair, bending forward, propping her head with her hands, pressing the temples as though she would press back the invading dread. Glancing suddenly at Henry's chair opposite, she rose and went to it, trying to be still, but a great longing for him, a great overmastering physical longing strained every fibre: she drew tight breaths painfully and rocked to and fro. When the clock struck twelve she went upstairs to the children's room.

The night light burned softly upon its high shelf, leaving the beds in shadow, mellowing the yellowish paint of the old ceiling. She took it down and stepped to the side of Dorcas' cot; the child slept calmly, breathing easily. She went to each bed in turn. There was deep rest here, but she might not stay: yet she waited after replacing the light. The baby stirred slightly — she went quickly to the cradle and lifted him out: she wrapped a blanket round him and carried him swiftly downstairs.

He whimpered a little. She began to pace up and down the dining room with him. Long after he had fallen asleep again she walked, swaying her body automatically, to and fro, up and down. At last she sank into the arm chair in a half stupor, but never relaxing her grasp of the child.

The light of the lamp burned low and became thick and smoky, then flickered out, leaving the room oppressive with fumes. The fire settled, the red glow died sullenly, and white ash lay thick on the bars of the grate; there was darkness. Dorothy still slept. When the dawn came grey creeping, thinning the darkness imperceptibly, it clung about her, showing her white face and fair hair in outline against the chair back. It dwelt upon the spread table, emphasizing its neglected hospitality: it gave an added desolation to the ash-strewn hearth, and a greater rigour to the lines of the family portraits. It permeated the whole room touching into a harsh significance one object after another. As it strengthened it lifted Dorothy's face from the shelter of the shadows. A strained expression grew more and more marked, the eyelids lifted slightly. When the actual sense of light penetrated to her brain she sat suddenly upright.

The brutal light struck and confused her for a few seconds. The cold and the pain of her cramped limbs brought recollection rushing back. Following upon a sense of the antagonism of the desolate room came the swift realization of her abandonment. It was absolute: there was no gainsaying her divination: the force of it swept through her overwhelmingly.

The light lay heaviest in a pale beam which crossed the couch and dropped to the floor below. It became more vivid, and she watched it from irritation, staring till it hurt her eyes. Then she moved and the baby woke. She carried him upstairs.

Select Bibliography

Boulton, J.T. (ed.), *The Letters of D.H. Lawrence* Vol I, CUP, Cambridge 1979

Corke, H., *In Our Infancy*, CUP, Cambridge 1975

E.T. (Jessie Chambers), *D.H. Lawrence: A Personal Record* (3rd ed.), CUP, Cambridge 1980

Nehls, E., *D.H. Lawrence: A Composite Biography* Vol III, University of Wisconsin Press, Madison 1959

Plowman, D., *Bridge Into the Future: the letters of Max Plowman*, Andrew Dakers, London 1944

Zytaruk, G.J. (ed.), 'The Collected Letters of Jessie Chambers', *D.H. Lawrence Review* XII Spring-Summer 1979

Archival sources

University of Nottingham Manuscripts and Special Collections

La D2/2 Portrait of Jessie Wood

La Ch 4/6 Typed copy of *The Bankrupt*

La Ch 84-5 Sketches by Jessie Wood

La H 27, 30, 31, 33, 35, 37-44 Postcards to May Holbrook

University College London Library Services

Letter from Jessie Wood to Max Plowman 22 January, 1936